THE RESURRECTION
OF THE ANIMALS

The Resurrection
of the Animals

Poems by

ANITA SKEEN

Luis:

I love how, periodically,
we cross each other's radar
screens and come back together
through language.

Fondly,
Anita

Michigan State University Press
East Lansing

♾ The paper used in this publication meets
the minimum requirements of ANSI/NISO
Z39.48–1992 (R 1997) (Permanence of Paper).

Michigan State University Press
East Lansing, Michigan 48823-5202

Printed and bound in the United States of America.

07 06 05 04 03 02 01   1 2 3 4 5 6 7 8 9 10

LIBRARY OF CONGRESS
CATALOGING-IN-PUBLICATION DATA

Skeen, Anita.
The resurrection of the animals: poems /
by Anita Skeen.
     p. cm.
ISBN 0-87013-609-7 (pbk.: alk. paper)
1. Nature—Poetry. 2. Animals—Poetry.
3. Human-animal relationships—Poetry. I. Title.
PS3569.K374 R47 2002
811'.54—DC21   2001007863

Book and cover design by Valerie Brewster,
Scribe Typography, Port Townsend, Wash.

Cover painting is a watercolor entitled
Jack Rabbit at the Back Door of Outer Space
©1992 by Carolyn Barford and is used courtesy
of the artist.

Visit Michigan State University Press on the
World Wide Web at:
www.msupress.msu.edu

for Gayle Davis and Fred Kraft,
whose love for me, and for animals,
made this book possible

ACKNOWLEDGMENTS

The following poems were previously published:

"After the Skirmish," Portraits (Douglas, Kans.: Kida Press, 1993); "Meltdown," *Mid-America Review* 19, no. 1 (1998): 92; "Hotel Room 5:00 a.m.," *The Atlanta Review* 2, no. 1 (1995): 20; "What Remains," *Clackamas Review* 3, issue 2 (fall 1999): 117.

I would like to express my appreciation to the Virginia Center for the Creative Arts for providing the environment that made a number of these poems possible, and also to the faculty and participants of the Ghost Ranch Creative Arts Workshop who both inspired and responded to many of them. I thank Ruth and Marion Clark for sharing their wonderful cabin at Silver Lake, Washington where others of these poems were written, and all of my friends who suffered through the various drafts, especially Ina Hughs and Mary Hayden. And Martha Bates, acquisitions editor at the MSU Press, who can spot a bad ending with her eyes closed. Finally, Beth Alexander, who has believed in me, and the poems, for twenty years.

Contents

THE RESURRECTION
OF THE ANIMALS

Taking in the Elements

Coyote Snow

All winter I've waited,
here in Portland,
for these trickster flakes
while every day rain
slops from the water-logged sky
and the temperature never drops
like it does back home
in Michigan, so fast and so hard
the day breaks in half
before your eyes.
Today's flurries lope
and lunge,
drunk on peyote wind.
I swear they almost grin,
white ice flashing.
Some float like down
from a million Snowy Owls
hoo-ing in their old growth woods,
nearly extinct too.
I fear I'm falling
seven floors
as I watch them plunge
and bite the street,
the pines, the concrete pots
and vanish. No text of tracks,
no thin skin hiding veins
of walk and highway.
No canceled school, yet
hope hangs visible as breath.

We're nervous, still.
Coyote snow, snow of the old tales,
kick up your ruckus
while we hunker inside,
wide-eyed as rabbits.
We count your whiskers twitching
at the burrow door.
Your furry paws scatter
the white dust.

Meltdown

It's the first of February and 40 degrees
in Michigan. Snow runs over roads and drives
like a broken egg. Listen: you can hear
the ground swelling with water, the trees
drowning. Roots are trying to come up
for air. Birds sail in on wings of sun.

Something has gone wrong at the core
of winter. Heat rises in the wrong places.
Each morning I wait for the north wind,
for the blizzard that wraps up the town,
the storm that makes the record books.
In the forecast: rain.

If the temperature dropped 20 degrees
there would be 20 feet of snow. My house
would lie like a low dune, the sea line
just beyond, surf frozen in its leap
toward light. There would be no drip
of gutter, no icicles ticking like bombs.

The Pond

Spring's showing off,
this last March day of winter,
flaunting all her promise
across the drowsy hills, flickering
in the redbud for any Doubting Thomas
still cowered indoors.
It's chilly, though, and the wind
prickles my fingers with porcupine quills
as I unloop the steel chain
from the gate, rust streaking my hand
like dried blood, and start down
to the pond. The cows have been, too,
sinking into the red clay, squishing
out craters of water opaque
as an earthy milk. I walk on
the grassy edge of a trail starlit
with bluebells. There's rustling ahead,
brush gossip, and plops into water
as the pond swallows.
The turtles heard me coming
and submerged, no interest in intruders,
no curiosity under their shells.
Farther on, two Canada geese
waddle my way and we pause
on the trail, facing like gunslingers
in the old west. They fire off
a Honk! Honk! before I can raise my camera
to take aim. But they're quick
on the wing, squawk off to the water

saying I'd better not follow.
They splash down among bleached stumps
jutting out, almost like shadows, each
of us this portentous day
caught briefly in the cross hairs
of the other's wandering.

Reading Margaret Laurence,
Thinking of You in Africa

It's April in Michigan and still the snow
comes. Tonight I drive home from class in a blizzard,
flurries attacking my windshield like an invasion
of albino insects. Their soft bodies splatter
against the glass, opening into frozen kaleidoscopes
till the wipers tilt them away. I feel trapped
in the truck cab, darkness everywhere.

In the stories of Margaret Laurence, men chop their way
through the lush underbrush, tall green fronds
surrounding them, heat rising with the day,
heat rising from the page. I long for something
green, some shoot or sprout puncturing
the brown winter thatch, some omen
for possibility. When the crocus in the front yard
unfurled their purple flags over snow,
rabbits chomped them to the bone.
I try to imagine the sweetness of such treats.

And you, in Africa now, bareheaded
and bare-sleeved somewhere in the Serengeti,
tracking something more peculiar than rabbit,
seeing color unlike anything in my upper Midwest.
I watch you crossing my mind's map
on your way to Mali and the elephants,
imagine you in a rattletrap jeep, brushing away
bugs frolicking in the air, whole nations surrounding you.

The light there, I think, must be brilliant,
space opening out in remarkable planes,
darkness, impossible to recall, even at night.

Taking in the Elements

To be lost is only a failure of memory.
MARGARET ATWOOD

Something as simple as the rain,
the surprise of its sweetness,
blackberries and cream,
as the season's first thunderstorm
pummels these hills.
I'm caught in the crossfire of water
and wind, whipped like loose laundry
as I break for the barn. Twenty years gone
from a life lived here:
the rut puddles in the red dirt road,
the crocus at the gate post.
This morning, a flurry of cherry
blossoms where, yesterday, only sky
trimmed the limbs. There's easy talk
at the table, the words in no hurry
to go anywhere. It's smell
that gives us memory back, they say.
This storm restores the April day
I splashed in a yellow slicker,
a quadruped duck, the ink
on my spelling paper fuzzing
into a field of blue dandelions.
So odd, having one foot in each time zone,
because of the nose. But it's also the cows
in their Rorschach suits, showing how,
so matter-of-fact, black abuts white,

not a crack in that Holstein geography,
those contrary countries patterning
into one skin.

Storm on the Mesa

1

From the portal of the wooden bunkhouse
I watch the sky darken. Clouds flower
into great hydrangeas. In the distance
veils of rain drape Pedernal,
displace the haze of forest fires
we've seen burning for weeks.
I think of Mrs. Noah scanning the skies
from her drifting bunkhouse, raft or coffin,
watching clouds like these surround her,
their deadly foliage spreading,
liquidation already underway.
But this is June, in New Mexico, only
half an inch of rain this year.
The sun flattens against our heads.
Prayers for rain go forth from the ranch
like doves.

2

My friends gather with me to watch.
All around us high red rock, crevice
and ledge, whorl and crest. The prows
of ships, the chimneys of stoves.
Blue black cloud against bright stone.
And then the crack, the jagged
snake speech of light, startling
our talk. Another snap

to the west, another south, the sky's
wiring exposed. A short circuit
in the late afternoon
gives us night.

3

The building speaks with the wind.
Doors murmur in their frames, windows
whistle and hiss. This conversation of plank
and rafter, nail and stud keeps us
still. We fine tune our ears.
Before Babel, all language was wind,
all creatures formed words
with its blustery vowels,
its intangible verbs.
This is a story of comfort,
not fear.

4

Finally, the rain. The mesas
around us dissolve in mist,
the temperature drops, the air
turns metallic and sharp.
I step off the porch
onto the blood-dark dirt, feel
the sting, the pricks
on my skin. Tongues
of lightning, tongues of wind,
the miraculous articulation of rain.
The storm spins a cloak

of moisture, a curtain of gauze,
between us and the heat.
Later, we will climb on our bunks
to sleep, to dream.

Going Home Again

The building's pink, the neon sign blue,
and inside, burgers arrive in cardboard Fords,
chocolate shakes lava-like in flow.
The waitresses wear pink, starched
white collars and neat cuffs, hair wild
as tumbleweeds. Above our booth,
between two Corvette hubcaps,
a poster of 1957 Chevies, which both
Fred and Mickey drove, and behind us,
pastel DeSotos from the same decade.
Whatever happened to DeSotos?
I ask Fred as *Run Around Sue*
spins out into the room and Gayle
says about the mound of onion rings,
These are as good as I wished them to be.
The black and white checked floor,
duck-tailed Elvis on an album cover
above the door, bored teenage couples
sprawled in the corner booth:
the Sweet Shoppe of my high school
days, the Shoney's I remember
on Saturday night. It is Saturday night,
the four of us parked at Don's Diner
on our way to play miniature golf.
It's not the fifties anymore;
we're in our fifties, on vacation,
already a bit unstuck in time.
These days Gayle plays pinball
on her IBM, not the ping and rattle

contraption just inside the entryway.
We're graduates of four small schools–
Concord, Muskingum, Earlham, Wabash–
laughing about our freshman beanies
and school songs, growing younger
with each quarter someone half our age
shoves into the magic slot
in the juke box.

August

Only two days away, August approaches
the house like news of the plague.
I feel its dark wings already
preparing to fold me
in their treacherous feathers,
all the while protesting they are bright
with heat, that they fly
the flags of summer vacation,
of endless leisure days,
that they ferry us
on soft gull wings across the lake,
resplendent with tilting sails.

But, I know August.

When August slams into town
with its suspicious laughter
and sleight-of-hand, I see that hand
unlatch its side show trunk, ease up the lid
on a coffin where days of sunrise
walks along the shore lie bled
of color, road maps for later excursions
waste away, starved and thin.

August says,
Hey, I'm just a tourist in this town,
tossing his trash from Burger King
on my lawn, *not to worry.*

August kicks open the schoolhouse door,
drags us in, hostage for another year,
leaves me with hunger not even the autumn
harvest can relieve.

Glen Huron, Late September

Napping with the old dog on the cabin deck,
I'm aware, off in the distance,
a chain saw rips through sunlight,

revving up, then withdrawing
like my brain snagging
on the same hardwood question.

On the wooded hill, I hear apples
drop one by one, tasty
and fat, and the last tomatoes glow
red like coals through thistle
and goldenrod.

It's a slow poke of a day,
this day.

I find that time is not the clock
I once thought, days ticked out,
chopped off and dropped into
history's pot, but a pond

where the water rises
and falls, rain and drought,
where brilliant fish pass
in hypnotic but disruptive waves

and frogs plop to the bottom,
webbed feet rupturing the muck,

dispatching puffs up through the clear
liquid, a murky Rorschach or aquarian
mushroom cloud.

The wind mounts an argument
against my back. Cedars and pines shake
their feathery heads in points
of fine distinction.

I listen, but have nothing
to say.

I feel old and forked
as the last carrot wrenched
from the earth, my fingers numb
with tingly sleep. My toes

try hard to snap off from their mother
limb, to crawl out on their own
like curious, naked babes,
tadpoles wriggling toward their first swim.

In the kitchen, someone concocts a soup
from beets, carrots, onions,
tomatoes and leafy summer growth.
The smell of herbs settles in the air.

A cabinet door slams.
Water sings

Becoming Haiku

How, in October, the world reduces
itself to a few syllables:

red leaf a slick spark,
frost sharp day. I come walking
early with the dog

straining at her leash,
nose poking at crystal grass.
But nothing shatters.

The morning sits still
as a room with a secret
where I find myself

shedding everything
but my bones and skin, this coat
the shape keeping me

intact: like the red
leaf, I break off from the branch,
become singular

and begin
my inward curl.

I Dream of Irene Running

on this, the first night of her absence
from the world, dream of her circling
the house, a small black and white blip

in the corner of my eye as she threads
among pines, the goldenrod, the dying elms
and cattails, hear thrashing in the weeds

where I know she has the scent of something
only she can smell, whiskered muzzle
twitching in the thatch of branches,

see her stop, look up, check out
where the family is, then lower her head
like the bull aimed for the matador

and again take off, full throttle
toward whatever might be just beyond the tree
line, the neighboring house, the edge

of her endurance, her paws drumming
a soft song on the earth's skin,
her old cocker body resurrected

with the joy of space and grass and no one
calling her name, calling her back
to a world of fence and collar,

as through my dream about splitting logs
while the first November snow falls
she runs in ever-widening orbits,

appearing like the moon, like a flicker
of memory, just when I had forgotten
she was there.

Two Poems for Two Years

NEW YEAR'S EVE: LAKE MICHIGAN

Though it's not the shortest day of the year,
the clouds stretch over this lakeside
house like the flannel blanket
I drop on the parakeet cage each night
for comfort and warmth.

What do I know of comfort to a parakeet?

The kitchen warms, warbles
with noise of dinner on its way.
Three voices harmonize.
I open the door to a porch
which in my childhood would have been

the veranda, and slip down to the lake,

snow flicking against my face.
At the trail's end,
hill, beach, waves continue
without demarcation, one from the next.
In the west, a rail of scarlet

runs the horizon splitting sky
and water, a bright ribbon
halving a Christmas gift.

I start to walk.

No searching for Petoskey stones
along the beach, white as a shroud.
Only hours of the old year left.
I do not want the new one.
As a kid, this was my abiding wish:
to stop time, to freeze the day,
until I could catch up. By first grade,

I was already behind. It's only gotten worse.

I want to push my hands
against this stiffening dark,
brace my feet on the insubstantial

ground, lean all my weight
against tomorrow's onslaught,
the Dutch girl, finger in the dike.

Two more steps west, my boot
fractures ice.

I'm out on lake, not beach. Water covers
my boot top, but when I put the next step down,
I'm solid again. I look back to see light
enticing from the kitchen window.

Like a white moth,
I turn back.

NEW YEAR'S DAY: LAKE MICHIGAN

All night the wind shook birch and fir
outside our window, their laments
for the last year tangling with my own.
They bend, they touch, they touch again.
Though it's too dark to see, I know

they find comfort in rubbing branch on branch,

touching needle to bark. The need to talk.
The wanting to take back.

When light allows me to look, I see
beach between hillside and lake.
Wind has blown away the snow fusing
water with sand, sand with slope.
Wanting to walk

that temporary strand, I dress and go down.
More wind than yesterday, last year.
The temperature's dropped. Rocks spill
like toys across the sand: chips of granite,
baked potato rocks, rocks lava black and smooth
as Santa Clara pots, fossils in Petoskey stones.

I start filling my pockets, remember Virginia
Woolf. I am not headed for the water.

Over the sea barricade and down the beach I go,
my back humped against the west wind.

Who hunts for Petoskey stones on a day like this?

My first act of the New Year:
rubbing my hands on the past, carrying stones
into the new day. When I straighten up,
at the seam between slope and beach,
two green Adirondack chairs, their wide arms

dusted with snow, snow banked in their sloping
laps, look out to the lake. Their arms touch
like uncertain lovers. They wait, fossils
of summer, imprinted on this winter day.

Here I stand, wanting
to take them in.

What Memory Makes It

What Memory Makes It

From a window in Vancouver
looking out through the evening light
toward English Bay, what I see
in the blue haze are the Smokies,

the Appalachians I abandoned,
each rise fainter than the one
before it, mountains sleeping
six deep. It's all dusted blue:

bay, hills, trees, even the glacial
snow nudging the blue clouds
near twin peaks called The Lions.
I prefer the old name, first name,

The Sisters, given by native people
before the British sailed in with heraldic
vision. Piano music floats nearby,
a song someone I love would know

by name. I can see gold stitching
through the blue, a thread in the water,
a guitar string reverberating under my skin,
along my blue veins, a minor chord,

the last note of that song I know
by heart but can't quite find.
This time of day the body quiets,
waits, listens, remembers.

Sky relaxes to the contour of dreams.
Water lies there, breathing,
longing, too, for touch—
a gull, a sailboat, a tremor of light,

a finger of wind.

My Brother Dreams His Way Home to the Woods

He is back in that house, he tells me,
back on the hill, dirt roads and old dogs
still everywhere. He stands in his bedroom,
a stranger's room these past twelve years,
looking through the one window, his hands
placed on the sash, his body leaning
into opening. But he does not feel
the wood, grained against his palms,
nor the sweetness of the mountain air
just after rain, when the window springs up.
He knows he is dreaming, he says, knows
when he wakes he will see palm trees
and highways, the white walls and shag rug
of his second floor apartment, hear
the air conditioner whir in the next room.
He knows he is not where he is, yet he looks
out the open window to the bank behind
the stone wall, to the trees, to the rope
clothesline, and the woods beyond. *Those trees,*
he says, *remember those trees?* How they wore
the snows of our childhood, how they were
our real home: furniture of boulder, carpet
of twig, curtain of vine. How we entered
our mother's walls only to change skins.
He stares at those trees, he tells me, afraid
they will vanish if he can't call their names,
afraid he will disappear before memorizing
their lines.

On the Wavelength

We could tell by the light, then,
when it was time to go home, time

to gather up the bats and caps, the jackets
shaped to bases, the nitroglycerin names

loose in the air. Or time
to disembark from the clean pine frame

of the new house going up, our Viking ship,
taking with us the splinters and resin

of conquest, the voyage dreamed
for the next day. The light dwindling

in the trees, the shadows masking our faces,
soon, only the voice visible nearby —

the quick-change artist of evening
already slipped into night —

and we, dirt on our knees
and shirt tails hanging, leaving

the blood brotherhood of neighborhood
no-goods until, again, the light

twitched its morning wink inside the window
saying *yes, now, friends*

are stirring in their houses, light
clicking through Venetian blinds, light

laying slats across linoleum floors,
light caught in the cobweb film of the grass,

waking bare feet, saying
play

Poem After Ironing

How easy just to sway there, moored
to the ironing board by the curled electrical
cord, pushing the iron through waves
of flannel, swells of denim, cruising along

the safe seas of rayon and silk.
I push the prow along plackets and cuffs,
into corners of collars, smothering
pockets and tucks.

I think of the pleasures
of soft cotton, the smell of sunshine
and late afternoon, a surge of steam
in the closed winter room:

on the rope clothesline of my childhood
I pinned my father's dark socks, always
in pairs, the blouses of my mother in colors
I would never wear, the print dresses

of my grandmother, silent and unstylish.
Last, I hung the sheets, matching
corner to predictable corner, and watched them
fill with wind like the sails of ships

in imagined scripts, carrying me off
over the hills of green water
swirling with trees, the paisley fish
leaping in our wake.

About Time

At sunup I walk to the island,
toward the bridge, to pick blackberries
when the Victrola trumpets
of three morning glories, surprising
as white flags, tune up an old song,
twining the melody around me,
making me see them
in pale blue, the summer morning
blue of the ones that dressed
the steep bank behind our house,
the ones I never noticed
until I was gone. They grew
wild among the weeds and brambles,
slips of sky nested in the brush.
Look in, these say, *look in,*
and I do, traveling a funnel
of daylight stars to a pale universe,
a blue hole turned inside out,
in which I see a child
and her grandmother,
my grandmother, struggling
in the scratch vines in hot July
sun to pluck ripe berries
from their clusters.
The two carry old pails, half-filled,
and the hats on their heads droop
like day old daisies. They stoop
and straighten, lean and
bend. Their wrists and ankles

burn with the criss-cross of thorn
tracks. The grandmother stops,
straightens, her hand at the small
of her back, wipes her face. She looks
toward the sky, into the unfurled fabric
of pure blue where, for a moment,
something seems to wink, to wrinkle.
And here I am, bending into
the white bell, my hands
cupped around it, eyes blinking.

Digging with Spoons

We bring plants to my grandmother's grave:
geraniums, because my mother always did,
marigolds because I think they will survive
if the others succumb, impatiens
because you are with me
and they are your choice.
Since I've been missing from this place
for thirty years, I follow the map
my mother gave me on the phone.
But I know this hill, the narrow road,
the smell of grass that always
conjures up the pink granite stone,
the bucket of water sloshing
in my adolescent hand, the trowel
mud-caked and bent. This morning
we realize we have no tools,
passing through this town on our way
from vacation to home, nothing
to spade up the hard earth and insert
summer bloom. But we have two wooden spoons
and a Swiss army knife, so we start to dig,
you hacking at the grass to the side of the stone,
me scooping a depression at the center,
in front. The dirt is stubborn, permanent
as loss. You go for water to the faucet.
I will a slot to open below the name,
a pocket to hold this overdue gift.
I curse the spoon, thinking, all her life,
how my grandmother made do with what she had,

never having the best or the newest
of anything. She would see this digging,
this chopping at the earth with a blunt blade,
as unremarkable, a matter of course.
She would give thanks for something
besides hands.

Linoleum

I want to say something about it, too,
Tess and Alice, about those dull floors
of the mountain homes, about the impossible
colors mashed into the mixture of cork
and linseed spread over a burlap backing:
the pea soup green of our 7th Avenue
kitchen, the baby turd brown of the church
basement, the crab shell salmon in the tiny
rooms rented from Miss Winifred Rew.
Turquoise and orange triangles on sky blue.
Mud grey stripes flecked with gold suns.
The floors I track on when I step
back in time, string mop in hand.
Cracked, glued down to warped boards,
rippling like a stream as it flows
through a hallway and three rooms.
I'm back in the house of someone's
great aunt in Kentuck, W. Va.,
something has happened, I can tell
from church ladies who bring
Jello salad and beans, chicken
and kale greens, high-backed chairs
rocking their creaky talk in the parlor,

my small body cold like this house
and low to the ground, but I see
linoleum swirling through the rooms,
me wading along it, into it,
voices high up like birdsong in lamps,
on mantel and clock, then somewhere
beyond linoleum, a woman cries.

Picnic

We take our lunch, and Spotty,
to your land, ten acres
where the dismantled cabin,
circa 1825, rises on concrete footers,
reconstruction begun, hauled log
by log from my home state.
The three of us walk the logging road,
through junked washers, an upended
chassis, into the ravine, hear
the mischief of a creek chattering
its path down, the headwaters
of the Mississippi, one of us jokes.
We spread the quilt, frayed and stained,
mystery in each cotton block,
flattening poison ivy and thorns, unwrap
the sandwiches and chips, watermelon
and red licorice. Spotty leans
into lunch, her leash looped
to a nearby tree. I take pictures
while the two of you laugh
and look for ticks, swat gnats,
then poke the leaves for snakes.
Women and food, I think,
talk about madness mixed in with
the grocery list. Last night,
over dinner, I spilled a secret,
surprising even me, into one of your laps.
I bring you both shirts with the logo
of a restaurant where, years ago,

we kept back terror with tacos
and guacamole. We lay this table
beneath dogwood and cherry, a patchwork
raft on a tangled and weedy sea,
the tide calm today, the wind still.
I eat more than I ever do at lunch.
Spotty gnaws on melon rind, vegetarian
bone. Praising the last cookie,
asking how you found the dowser
who predicted your well, we pack up
paper and foil, free the dog
to sniff suspicious growth,
our baskets lighter as we maneuver
through snarled brush.

Salvage

for Peggy Mucklo

Inside the chain link fence, padlock
the size of a strongbox, refugees
of demolition and urban renewal
camp out on the trampled grass:
chunks of granite, some polished,
some rough; thin slate from roofs,
thick slate from floors; church pews
10 feet long that curve like a highway.
A stained glass window, Christ's arm
missing; wrought iron fences
and wooden spindles. We come
for a clawfoot tub for your cabin,
find a collection lined up
like race cars for the gun.
Some are long and low, boat-like,
others squat and solid,
more practical than aesthetic.
I try out one, clambering
over paving stones and marble slabs,
lower myself in, settle back.
Not a bad fit, I tell you,
deep enough for a good soak.
You try another, though rain
collects in the bottom,
drain plugged with rust.
We measure lengths and widths,
amazed at subtle differences
in the porcelain fleet, continue

among toilets and sinks,
handsome mantles, barrels of nails
and bins of doorknobs. I choose
the crystal one, fluted and heavy,
turn it in the light, catch lavender
and blue tints. I think how time
turns in peculiar ways, you
and I friends for a quarter century,
here in the Virginia sun, poking
among remnants of other lives,
loss and dislocation everywhere,
while we finger brass andirons
and speak of my visit next fall.

Loose Ends

after Richard Hugo

That's where I'm writing from today:
you'd laugh, I know, then ask if I'm hiding out
in a nobody-thinks-twice-about mountain town
down some West Virginia dirt road
or a country-western bar on the back side
of the tracks in Wichita. Maybe a cut-rate
haircut place in Meridian Mall?

Not so. It's the dark side
of the moon, I think, though the ground
blazes diamond-bright and January wind
conjures snow into dust devil ghosts.
How can the sun be this cold, splinters
of light driving into my eyes?
I remember when I was a kid, those

summer days boredom made us all crazy,
and the spark of a wrong word set off
war. My friend and I took Octopus Tree
where, from the high branches, we hurled
twigs and limbs at the tribe below.
One stick aimed from ground-level snagged me
in the left eye. The whole tree leapt
inside the small universe of my eyeball.

I ricocheted to the earth, loose
like a marble in a pinball game,
to run, furious at the boy

with a pitcher's arm and my mother,
already poised by the open door,
hands on her hips, never understanding
about pocket rocks or pokeberry ink
or the usefulness of persimmons.

Why, now, will I try to explain to you
the view from the tree's attic, how I could see
Elk River threading through the green maze,
the railroad tracks beginning and ending
in stories I could never know?
Sometimes, wandering alone,
looking for chunks of coal or pancake
pennies along the steel-blue rails,
I'd hop from tie to tie to tie, naming
each one a place to go, hoping
a thing I'd never imagined
lay glinting ahead.

Water Words

If I lived by the shores of this lake
for the rest of my life, I would learn it,

this language of waves. Ducks traverse
on its syntax of dip and furrow.

The language is simple: we spoke it
before birth. When we opened out

into surgical steel, flourescent light,
fingers suffocated in a second skin,

we lost touch, we left it behind,
vanished with our memory

of rocking through water, curled
like a cashew in the mother's pod.

Late at night, in darkness, by this lake,
I feel it working its way back, its way in.

I bend to the water's edge
listening, forming the sounds

with my ears. I remember how
noun was a beating, steady and rhythmic,

verb a cradle of flowing: whisper, lick,
tickle, rush, gossip, rustle, murmur—

my body a quarter moon in the womb's sky,
my fists tugging starfish from the tide.

Barges

Out of my window passing in the night
I can see the barges' flickering light...
CAMP SONG

For eleven days I've watched from my high window
the boats on English Bay. They travel on this grey plain
from Vancouver to Seattle and Victoria, to Alaska
and places I can't name. Sharp sailboats circle
like white-finned sharks. Ferries plod along beside them,
and cruise ships cut through the water with their steel
laughter, haughty in their racks of lifeboats and jazz
band playing on the upper deck. But it's the barges
I watch for, binoculars skimming over pleasure boats
and tankers. What is this romance with the barge,
rectangular bin sunk almost to water level with its weight
of lumber and sand, boxes and crates, work horse
among the painted ponies and rodeo mares?
When I was a child I watched the river near my home
carry the burden of coal – six, seven, eight barges long,
the tug sputtering like it might go under, the fractured
heart of my mountain transplanted to another state.
No hulls with colored wings, no speedboats
pulling skiers, no sternwheeler of gamblers, cards
flying before gunshots. Only the barges, steady
and dependable, ran the river, some tangible sadness
in their silent passing, north and south, some sense
in me of the life of work, simple and necessary.
Now I watch them in another country, sunset
streaking by like a comet, as I sit at my desk
to write, my cargo of words floated on lines

as on a river, the heart blasted and mined
into dark, hard rocks, each one
capable of fire.

And How the Light
Came Up Behind Us

To Begin Again

you will need these things:

the love of a dog,
fur against your chest
at night, someone
to howl for you

constellations of needle
and leaf
or the arms of someone
tall to shelter you,
to be able to see
light beneath the green
skin, to feel light
in the veins of your hands

a post card from a place
you've never been

a room in your heart to store
the past, the door
locked, the key
a spark which can ignite
even the rain

the comfort of waves,
elastic conversation
of water and rock

the silence to follow.

Adirondacks

Yes, there are mountains
by that name, deciduous upheavals
of the earth's surface
shaped when something ancient
and great burrowed its way
below New York state.
But in my landscape the word
names chairs, broad boards
fanning into slanted backs,
wide arms extended in trance.
Mugs tilt comfortably on the plank
shelves while fingers trace
lives in the grain.
The seat, deep enough
to sink into, confirms
the futility of legs, absurdity
of mobility. To rest,
therefore, to be.
At Ghost Ranch, the Adirondacks
set up colonies: beneath
the cottonwood, plumed
and loose like a funnel cloud;
in the orchard; outside
the library. Theirs is the repose
of poets, turning the line.
Some days the chairs migrate,
heading south with the heaviness
of cows. If speech were theirs,
we would hear in their sway the long song

of lumber, the torture of boards
separate from their trees.
But they are stoic.
They remain tight-lipped,
tight-limbed. I have sat
in their slatted laps
under desert sun,
below snowy starlight.
I have reached out
from their shelter in exposure
to all weathers. I have felt
their bones startle, felt them
listen with open mouths
when I said *yes.*

Fire Trees

Spark of leaf, flame
of branch,
smoke-curl clouds
rise over hills
smoldering
orange. Long line
of birch,
the forest spine,
bleached by dry heat
like desert bones,
the train I ride
a sun-struck stream
channeling north
beneath crackle
of maple, blaze of beech.

Look: sumac strikes
another match.

Autos Under Snow

after James Wright

Just off the highway to Spokane, Washington
the rows of autos hunker
under snow, ranges
of chassis and axle
permanent as the Cascades.
I think of the combined mileage
of the stalled odometers,
the road tales of the tires,
liaisons formed in the back seats.
In this wilderness, stillness
like a caught breath.
No whir of engine cranking, no grinding
of gears, no honking or rock music
blaring from the cracked heart.
Small varmints reside
under hoods, in metal hollows,
nest in leather.
Under snow shrouds,
bright blue snaps in the sunlight,
a red fender flares, yellow
pokes up an open trunk.
Lilies of the field
in this soft garden, magic
beans hibernating
in winter pods.

Myth Making

Wandering the night
unable to sleep
I walk to the window
to check on the snow:
a forecast of ten inches,

which I can't believe,
hangs in the air.
I flip on the porch light,
look out toward the lake
which I can't see.

The night sits black and empty
as the old felt boards
in my Sunday School class
before Noah, then the ark
were slapped against them.

Then, from the sky,
flurries frisk toward earth:
all the stars of heaven,
unleashed from their constellations,
seeking a different story.

Marie's Trees

We dug them,
in the ripe spring,
when they unfurled
green flags
in surrender
or welcome,
the thin maples
rooted at acute angles
on the steep bank.
A neighbor's cat
curious about
spades and mattocks,
buckets and bags,
tumble-grinned
through our ankles,
among hands, blitzing
and vanishing,
a feline Phoenix rising
from the scrap leaves
while we potted
and packed.
We drove them
fifty miles, rolled
them into fresh
holes, staked them
upright. Mounding dirt
at their base
I remember
the young calico

we had in Kansas who went
missing.
We gave her up
for dead, though
no body lay
in the roadway.
Twelve days later
she returned,
one dimensional thin,
and never again
left the back yard.
We think she got trapped
in a workman's truck,
taken across town,
had to whiff her way
home with whisker radar,
green eyes
plotting
the calculus
of paws.
I push hard
on the dirt around
this tree,
kneading
it to rise, imagine
some dawn while I'm still
sleeping, a leaping
of squalling
leaves
into the air,
roots
ripped loose,

dangling,
the kidnapped saplings
headed home.

After the Skirmish

for Jeanine

It's more than a puzzle to you now
how this young weed of a woman who shares
your house grew from the diapered seedling,
the green nubbin, the wire-fenced sprout.

Where did she learn the words
she hurls at you, the Goliath of her life,
from the sling of her needs, the hard leather
of her wants? She can't conceive

of memory's tricks, how the film clips
click on unpredictably, how nothing can ever be
edited out. She can't feel your heart
swallow itself when, at midnight,

and with the hall light still on,
the phone kicks you from sleep,
her stone to the forehead
arrowing straight toward its mark.

Mother, for her, is the warning
on the label she won't care
to read, the treacherous question
phrasing itself in the room next to hers.

Daughter, for you, is the glittering box
that keeps ticking, the mushroom, luscious to look
at you think you recognize but aren't sure,
and don't find described in any of your books.

Hotel Room, 5:00 a.m.

Around me the sounds of rented space:
in the hall a key clicks
and voices explore the intimacy
of anonymous lives.
The clock radio on the bedside table,
set to someone else's schedule,
announces a change in the weather
while the heater hums on, not hopeful.
I see through the gauze curtains
the night lights of the city, offices
abandoned and silent, streets
wary and braced for surprise.
In this building, someone dreams
of a child four states away, a woman
waits for her lover on the phone
to his wife upstairs, a bellhop
sets down a man's luggage
outside the door next to mine,
not knowing what he toted
down the carpeted hall,
what outrageous joy
or grief may be contained
in such tight space.

Morning, After Rain

I'm used to the earth plump, white,
the world in loose definition

out my window after midnight
storms. But this morning, the air

drips grey, sodden, and the pools
on the soaked deck mirror

my face. The birds return
with their pointy chirps

and the geese honk by on their trail
over shards of ice. It's all

too sharp, these needlepoints of noise,
stab of branch and corner of roof,

crocus piercing the dirt. Who can say
what questions dart through the blank

sky like sudden crows, what blades
were honed undetected under snow?

Peaks of Otter

They rise like the mountains children draw:
peaks rounded, forest green crayon
between the lines. The sky swirls cerulean,
though no round sun with spikes hangs
in the upper corner. Like children, we're drawn
to the water, the cascade hike winding us down
through wildflowers and ferns, timbered steps,
and a red shirt hangs like a lantern
on the limb of a dogwood. It flickers
in the spring light. We descend toward
the conversation of water and rock,
our words spilling onto moss, our sentences
a rope ladder we cling to.
Like the otter we never see,
we wade into the cold stream, stones slippery,
footing precarious. So cold it cramps my toes,
the water teases around sharp surfaces,
into pools and eddies, rushes down
over ledges like liquid light.
I want to drop my body into the current,
feel it become loose as liquid, feel it
take in the stones and flow through
tangled branches and cones. I watch
my body spreading into the water,
losing syntax, and taking motion
as its only language,
leaving my friends on the lush bank
startled and speechless
as I slither beyond sight.

Letter While Driving

As I rise on the road,
the fog descends, denying
my right to know by sight
where I am. I find these hills

a comfort, how they allow
rivers into their private
hollows, the moon to spend
the night above the ridge
before traveling on,

unlike the north where I go,
where land flattens out,
the hard line on a monitor
reporting a stalled heart.

Through the fog, headlights
approach, twin moons
flying too low, reckless
in their tandem brightness,

astral renegades
softening my lane ahead.
The hills open up to take me in,
then close behind me quiet

as thought. I grip the wheel,
both hands pressed to its curve

and firmness. It's touch
that keeps us steady
in all things.

Rock of Ages

In Arches National Park, rocks bend
and twist into shapes impossible for stone,
balance Gibraltar on a pencil point,
burn like candles in the desert light.
We take a trail toward Red Cliffs.
It's late in the day. We're alone.
We track through what could be ocean
sand, except for prickly pear
and sagebrush on this beach,
then follow the trail up over the fallen
face of the cliff, chunks of mesa
dumped everywhere. I follow you
behind a slab the size of a billboard
to see the mountain split like a log,
a clean cut almost all the way through.
In the cleft there's room to walk,
to stand, to lean back against the cool
tight skin of the earth. I go in
as far as I can, half the rock
in darkness, half in light.
In this breath of a space,
we relax, lie like lichen
against the cliff. We imagine
the markings above cut
by women like ourselves,
out for a walk, out for company
in the miles of silence.
Not to mark history,
or carve art,

but to hear their own voices
touch song in the heart of the rock
as they talk.

And How the Light Came Up behind Us

for Lynn Robbins

We set out later than we should
to walk this canyon rim, two miles
around both Tower Loops, ruins
of the Anasazi trimming the trail.
The sun's going down,
we're going out to watch
the last light set candles
in the silent windows, strike
sparks on ancestral rock.
We whisper, though no one else
is near. But others come:
the raven who watched us pitch
the tent flies low, picking up
friends. Three roost on the Square Tower
when we arrive. Lizards cross our path,
frequent as handshakes at reunion.
One lets me look him
in the eye. He'll not be the first
to blink. We stop and look,
stop and look, stop and stop.
The sun's dropped down behind
the rim as we walk on:
Steep Trail. Use Caution.
the sign warns, and it's getting dark.
We didn't bring a flashlight.
It seemed a violation.
We slip down to the canyon floor,
wind through boulders

like water seeking water.
When the moon and stars arrive,
we sit on a fallen log
and tell our stories.
A rabbit brings his story, too,
but hurries on. It's time to go,
we know. The darkness deepens.
So up the trail we climb,
and at the top, head out across
a plain of sandstone toward the tent.
But somewhere there's a light–
behind us–yet less than a quarter
moon. We stop to look.
No other hikers
coming home, no headlights
on the gravel road above.
No one but us.
We move along, joined by
two shadows, though it's not
the moon's bright beam
that guides us home.

Listening to Traffic

So many plots humming by in glass and steel,
in darkness. How is it in a different life?

The silence of closed fists, of still water?
What currents do they ride in the swell

of noise that washes this room, what
longing for perfection?

Each car bears its carnival
of the ordinary, headlamps beamed out

in gratitude or loss. The wheels
sing: joy, joy in simply going round.

The Store of Things

While You Sleep

These mountains sleep
side by side, nesting shoulder
along shoulder, knee behind knee,

asking for my hand to reach out
through this cabin window,

to reach toward the blue arc
of the hip, the green lift of the breast,
to lose my hand in the channels
of river, my fingers tickling in streams.

In this first light I can barely

call light, how the mist
rises from their curves, how their forms
quicken as I reach
toward them, how they reel in

breath when my hand brushes
trillium and fern, my fingertips
hush over moss. My hand flutters

like moth wing, like falling dogwood,
among the spring leaves
slips under the rocky ribs of creek
beds, ascends the explosion of rapids

in my cupped hand. Damp
and pungent, my hand returns to me,
fingers tracing my open lips

as these hills open to rain.

Mid-Sentence

I sit hooked
by a cord to a black box
which, like a ventriloquist,
throws your voice
into this dim closet
of a room, into my anxious
life, your voice which
is not here
but is, your body
years away. I see you
in the kichen
stroking butter on your toast
as we talk

or in your office holding out
a paper to a man
who walks into the space
of this call
never knowing what
questions pick their way
along the wires, practiced
as acrobats, what words
abort in his presence,
what small thefts
he commits
though he offers a hand,
empty, seconds after
you hang up.

Light and Shadow

It's an almost-full moon, an almost-dark
night. No one on the beach
but me and across the bay a light
I take for the evening star
poking through crimson clouds
becomes a blinker on a tower
once the sunset gives in
to the blue-black backdrop.
The stars stay distant, only a memory
of constellations I named
above mesas in the high desert
just two weeks ago. They've shifted
places, appearing where I don't expect,
and an Adirondack chair, same
as the one I nested in at the ranch,
waits like a well-trained puppy
beside a dune. The slice from the moon
that makes it not quite full, the rush
of the waves that say this sand's
not desert but a shore, the way the stars
congregate in this sky to knock me
off-guard, some other time
reverberating in each presence,
my own ghost reclined in the wooden chair,
head tilted toward the heavens,
hearing your voice in the surf.

What, in a Moment

After hard rain, darkness
only a breath away, we walk
the polished streets down
to the Tennessee River.
Headlights hold back in fog
like difficult questions.
I hear rain falling
into trees we walk beneath,
the persistent dripping
random and unrhythmic.
When wind snatches
the branches, small storms
shake loose, arguments
among leaves. We continue
through the park,
the water nearer, flickers
on the far bank
like misplaced stars.
At the water's edge,
no bench to rest on,
the grass too wet
to sit on, mosquitoes
hungry and contentious,
we stand watching
a single duck
slash its arrival
across the dark stream.
There's a rip
in the rippling silk,

transitory, quick
as a finger snap.
The river, unlike the heart,
makes nothing of the wound
and moves on.

A Matter of Perspective

To survive is sometimes a leap into madness.
JOY HARJO

Think of Emily Dickinson, shut up
in that New England town, with a woman
she would have called lover, called
harbor, married to her brother and living

next door, but in another galaxy.
And your own past self, planted
like a blue-black petunia in a windowbox
while she with the velvet tongue walks outside

with another woman, their fingers together
a lattice of bright stars. They're gone
from your heaven, those stars
you used for charts as you crossed

the difficult landscape
of night, whether the noon sun
was overhead or the trickster moon,
white as a virgin, luminous as a lie.

Think of the moon, herself a victim,
speaking only through the sun's borrowed
light. She is neither star nor sun,
but a third body, burning

in the dark like a third eye,
the one too primitive to trust,

the one whose arm you have already
placed your hand on, wanting

to write legend on this wild night.

After Landing

It was sudden lift-off
when you said
I love you,
turned at the airport
check-in where people exploded
like popcorn between us
and I lost you
down a concourse
not my own.

Not the details of the jet's wings
dipping right, then left
over Niagara, not the conversation
with a friend about loss,
not the photos I found
in the mail when I returned home
or how the yard greened
in my absence

are what I call to tell you,
but how each turn
of my head refracts you
in the light, how each word spoken
in my presence resonates
with the possible,
how the ordinary furniture
of the day, at any moment,
might take flight.

The Store of Things

*Neurobiologists speculate that memory, like pain, does
not reside in a single place, but floats like smoke through
the body.*
SANDRA ALCOSSER

Where is it you are camped
tonight? Just off the pulmonary artery,
the islets of Langerhans, on the banks
of the alimentary canal?
When I find myself
off balance, I know you
are on the move. I put up
Keep Off! signs in danger spots:
tear ducts, eardrum, the steep cliffs
of the heart from where a fall
is always fatal. You're as hard
to track as the Abominable Snowman.
I hear your calls, like Coyote, echo
from clavicle to sternum, through the canyon
of the abdomen.
Now, there, your raven wings
flap up toward the rafter of ribs.
There's a stutter in my breath.
You are loose in my chest
like a bad cough, rumbling along
somewhere out of sight,
causing an outburst at exactly
the wrong time. I think
you are headed nowhere
in your tinker's wagon, rickety

wheels just around the next
vertebra, maybe under the patella.
You've stopped to gather wood,
knowing how to keep us both
warm when the forecast is fierce.

Thinking of You, at the Piano

Solid, I think. Permanent. The first
thing I see when I enter the room,
marooned on the island of Persian rug,
its ebony curves tugging like shoreline.
Black keys, white keys mute
till you swim to them, lower
your hands, stroke ivory, touch
sound. You speak the language
of strings, catch the voice
of the stream remembering,
the narrative of crystals
whispering in clusters underground.
A season melts, then freezes.
Fast. I hear stories of stones
traveling through ponds, something
alive diving from a high place.
Someone dances up a flight of stairs
(or stars?), dances down, toward
me, takes my hand. A voice calls
from geography with no name.
Finally, the darkness:
inseparable from the light.

Driving North

I have strung your number from pay phones
throughout the Midwest on the long drive home,

trying to go the distance, learning
the real distance too late.

The day rings flat as a wrong number
and threatens snow. What words
do I think I can say

that will unwind the tangle
between us, a twisted phone cord?

The voice in my head says *keep talking*
keep talking as if the right words
clicked in the right nicks

could pop the combination lock
on your heart, flick it open

in my palm. Once, I think,
there were such words.

I fingered them, inattentive
to the ticking of my own
heart. What do I want

your words, disembodied
in the rooms of my ear, to give
me back? A few hard syllables

to shatter the heart's longing?
Oh, words that lead us into passion

and to grief. Words like leaves
in this winter season. Words

poised like rabbits before the headlights
of the ringing phone.

Golden Ponies

They stand head to head in a field of snow,
coats like winter grass
shaggy and short.

I see them from my red truck
traveling I-40 east to Amarillo,
mesas and turquoise receding,
steel and glass the day's drive ahead.

I think of the two of us, standing
this morning that way, a moment before
the sharp turn, door closing,
ineptness of ending.

I would have wished for the grace
of these ponies, for their symmetry
in a landscape of singulars,
for their steady breath.

Two ponies bright
against the tin badge sky.
Dark clouds in the west.

Two ponies, nothing between them.

The Moon, the Waves, the Fire

In separate sleeps, we dream.

My dream is of the moon passed
among the soft branches of the tall pines
like a white pebble
passed through the linked fingers
of women.

Mine is of the fire arguing
with itself, spitting into the air
loose words, hot and terse.
They burn out
like stars.

Mine is of the waves.

I cannot see your dream

but I hear your breathing crash
against the room's silence,
throwing up rocks in a stone offering.

I think the sky of your dream
is moonless, lit by heat lightning
twitching like the digital face
of your clock, figures
constantly in countdown.

In what place do our dreams
intersect
like our bodies
tangled in night's sheetscape?

I sit alone on my dream's shoreline
warmed by fire, comforter
in the dark's cold.
The water speaks a language
in which I am no longer fluent

but the cadence sends me back
to a sleep

where the moon
comes swinging up the path,
a lantern
in the hand of someone
I remember
I came here to meet.

In Oklahoma, of All Places

A kiss has nothing to do with sex,
you tell me, surprising my lips
with yours, your arms
folding me into your heart.
I can't speak, of course,
but feel my heart climb
like a full moon on a cloud
littered night, like a duck
startled in the marsh.
Your hands spread
across flannel, fingers
press into plaid.
Like comets' tails
they arc across my shoulders,
plunge, avoiding the trap
of the breast
pockets, rendezvous
third button from the top.
Now the moon, round
and pearl-faced, slips
through a slot in the dark.
Whole constellations change
configuration, can't decide
which legend to be part of,
can't remember what distance
to keep from earth.
A kiss has nothing
to do with sex, you repeat,
your hands unbuckling

Orion's belt.
Bodies collide, skies
above the red dirt
forever altered.

What Remains

Tonight you won't be home,
though I begin to watch
my watch, lay aside a book,
check the fridge for possible dinner.

I drink iced tea this hot May day.
Iris cut from your garden this morning
flame on the glass-topped table,
their sweetness sticking to the air.

The silence of departure
surrounds me. Outside a dog
barks, a mower scatters clippings
like last night's words.

Fragrance of bled grass rises,
sifts through the screen.
In Spring Hill Cemetery
every Decoration Day my father

slashed fresh growth releasing
that same scent. The blades
of the push mower whirred,
the racket of winter's passing.

Voices distant, laughter
spilled into evening
from another plot, affirmed
the living always among the dead,

the way they tend to memory,
how absence fits the hands like work
gloves, clatters to concrete
like a dropped spade.

This Time in Virginia

I've come out to the gazebo to watch
the full moon rise above the staggered roofs
of the barn. Another state, another moon,
and yet another train clatters along nearby tracks.
A train can do it every time – bring up loss
like an image in developing fluid –
the clank of absence ever present in its passing.
You said last week we would soon watch
the same moon from different landscapes,
plugged into its light from separate
sockets, and so I flip the switch,
my darkness coming hours before yours,
leaving on the porch light
as I turn in to bed.

The Resurrection
of the Animals

The Resurrection of the Animals

For most of them, no waiting,
no slow lifetimes packed away
underground.

They do not trouble
with theological questions:
Will I recognize my family
on the other side?
Which of my sins will count most?
Where is Hell, really?

In that irreversible snap
of transition between the chasing of something—
a scent, a memory—across the highway to the impact

of metal and pressure of tires,
the hound's curiosity
splinters into spectrums of light,

the body dropping, useless
now. In autumn the blood of the dog
flows back in the black-red

growth trimming the road.
The lamb, the calf, the hog,
peering from the slatted, rattling truck

at an awkwardly jolting world, flee
with the butcher's blow

into the unfenced, unpenned
night. While their bodies are carved

for the table, they pasture
among stars. In winter the fleece
of the sheep lies banked in their former fields.

The rabbit, the coyote, the deer – all
the earth's hunted – romp, sudden
herds of wind, when the bullet

lasers through their lives.

They are not asked to forgive
their enemies. They make the air
electric as they pass.

Planting Chrysanthemums on the New Grave

In this warmest fall I can remember
I take the pot of chrysanthemums
sent to me during an illness outwitted,
and carry them to the fresh dirt, clods
still moist. The petals radiate, rich brown
with gold centers, the sun ringed by slender velvet
slices of love's questions. I jab my fingers
into the earth, scoop out a round depression,
thinking how this dirt crumbles the same way
as the stale bread I leave out for the birds.
In each lump are worlds of microscopic life,
their universe spilled out in my flat palms.
I dust them off against my jeans,
an indifferent God, and place the clump of roots
snugly in the hole, careful to pack them
tightly for protection against November
frost, due any night.
I make small six inch pits to circle the plant
and insert bulbs – tulips, daffodil,
so there will be color in the Spring,
the hues of sunrise bursting only inches
above ground. I smooth the dirt again,
crushing lumps with my fist,
squeezing hard enough to turn these lumps
to lignite, to coal, to diamond,
its many facets blaring expectation.
Last, I pour the water from the can
over the small mound, watching it disappear
quickly as a face I thought

I'd never forget. I press my hands
against the damp earth for the last time.
The prints of my hands hold shallow pools,
evidence of contact between absences.

Upstairs in the Storm

This must be how the fledgling feels
gripping the elastic limb of poplar or birch,
lights flashing like photographers'
bulbs, 2:00 a.m. darkness blitzed into day.

Tossing in the heat on our coverless beds,
our only warning a stiff breeze,
we hear papers flapping from the desk like gulls
startled on the offshore rocks or doves released

in a gesture of peace. Next the crescendo
of wind, waves of storm pummeling the house
anchored in woods. I leap up to slam shut
the windows, salvage items blown to the floor,

see lights flip on downstairs, and just as quickly,
flicker off. Now the only light's the flickering
neon out among the trees, a Morse code
of storm script I can't read. High up

with the acrobatic trees, in my nest
of a room, when thunder smacks
against the barricade of night
and lightning strikes nearby,

I think again of that small bird, wings
opening for the first time into the bedlam
of the world, the egg cracking,
light bolting in.

Another Story About Stars

I watch them, on a night
still as held breath,
above the ruins at Hovenweep
where ancient ones sat on rocks
and mesas inventing the lives
of stars, the legends of dark.
But here I am
by a tent
beneath the same stars,
the same light that sparked
their tales urging me
to speak: to say
that these flickers
must be the eyes
of creatures
gone from among us,
coyote and snake,
lizard and loon, rabbit
and wolf, looking back,
like Lot's wife, these pillars
of fire,
sniffing the bent bush,
the snapped twig, watching
to see who goes where.
When light
haloes the earth's
rim, their eyes nod to sleep.
As day retires, they rouse,
seers into long grasses

and arroyos.
This July night
one steady eye finds mine,
each of us singular
in such vast space,
neither
of us able to turn away.

Evensong

For years, as I drove the roads
in Kansas and light took leave
of the vast flatness, I watched
the cows, rock solid and orderly,
sway home through the green
undulations toward a barn
I couldn't see, a pasture beyond
my knowing. Tonight, at Silver Lake,
light pulls its usual tricks.
I watch the ducks, bobbing
and self-important,
sail like a small navy
to the island where they nest.
Some chatter, some quarrel,
some reserve comment, like cows.
They float past Canada geese
arrowing the opposite way, necks
curled in silent questions.
The lake plays in the light
like silk, shimmers metallic
in the lining of the loose waves.
Above it all, suddenly, dark wings
bank, dip, coast under rosy clouds,
the flapping too huge for raven
or duck. The bird drops
like a stone, a kite in a tailspin.
I expect to hear glass shatter,
smashing of feather and bone,
but only talons break

the liquid plane, struggle
and splash. The white neck
lifts, the head rises,
it gains height, an eagle
gripping a fish, taking
the shortcut home.

A Sadness

For Emily Kilby

Although no chirping springs
from the cage where, for five years,
the parakeet who flashed like green
neon opened the day with song,
in the cage of my brain she still extends
her wings, leans into manic flight.
Behind my eyes, the whirring
of yellow-green. Bird-talk at the feeder
excludes me, foreign chatter.

Not a big loss, some would say.
Not an important death.

Two days before her light-as-a-soul
body toppled from its perch
in permanent stillness, you wrote
to say your bird, left alone
in the house outside his cage
while you went off to a blues concert,
dashed himself, driven by some unfathomable
fear, against a window. You found him
limp below the sill. Guilt battered
your heart like the trapped bird.

Think of the small creatures we take
into our lives, the gift of their non-human
presence: the rabbit's ear lifted
to the sound we don't hear,

the whiskered twitching of the gerbil
in his wobbly wheel, the flourescent notes
of tropical fish as they swim
their unfinished symphony.
The unremarkable way, like the air
we inhale, they sustain us,
our struggle for breath
when they're gone.

Tales

For Carolyn Barford

On Sunday morning, instead of church,
our congregation heads toward Box Canyon.
You and I veer off from the others,
bound for Kitchen Mesa,
across desert toward the red cliffs.

You've done this before, know
secrets carved into rocks.
You name the petroglyphs
you've seen, talk of ones
Jim has told you how to find.

I'm eager to climb these slabs,
to feel my boots grip the ledge,
grab gnarled juniper to hoist myself
higher. We slip through barbed wire,
skirt prickly pear, hunt for

an opening among cholla and sage.
I keep looking at rocks:
boulders blazing with light,
Stonehenge configurations at the base
of the cliff, pebbles to fit

my pocket or palm. One of these,
slick as red water, lies a few feet away.
I cross, bend to take it from the sand,

then hear the noise:
    cicadas, cicadas, cicadas

But that can't be, here on the ground.
It goes off again
just as I think
    rattler
and see coils undulating under rocks.

I leap away, give up my rock
and we go on, a bit sobered, a bit
more alert. At the trailhead,
we start up loose rock, reach
the face of a huge cliff.

I look up and think of Moses,
though these tablets give no laws.
Up we go to a narrow ledge, then slip
along. I tell you about my fear
of heights and how my mother once got stuck

on the stairs of The World's Largest
Hand Dug Well in Greensburg, Kansas,
paralyzed, unable to go up or down,
and my travels with a friend who froze
on the cliffs in Baja and had to be slid down

to the sea, eyes locked shut.
We climb awhile, come to a place
where the ledge breaks off.
If we go on, we have to hug the cliff,
our hearts beating against its heart,

our feet suctioned to rocks.
We both know the story of a climber
who died here. We decide not to go on,
sit down to rest before we descend.
You tell me how you imagine

earlier Indians perched here,
guarding the canyon, doing whatever
watchers do. Then, above us, we see
tracks of elk, of deer, carved into rock,
a six-toed paw print, the delineation

of open hands. We stand, startled,
place our palms to the palms
of the rock. We find marks for counting,
slanted lines we have no explanation
for, something that looks like a fish

so far from water. I call it mesa trout.
No, you scoff, it's jackrabbit at
the back door of outer space.
It's time to go down. You lead,
stop abruptly. There's another snake,

much smaller, sunning himself
across the ledge, the only way
down. We wait. The snake waits.
You think he's another rattler
until we see his tail, bald and silent,

As he sidles parallel to the cliff,
giving up nine-tenths of the path,
we tell him about our families,

what we're looking forward to next week,
decide it's okay to share. We walk

beside him, carefully, remind him that we know
it's his mountain, that we're only tourists
here. He slides into a jar lid size hole,
a patterned conveyor belt,
as we pass. I look back to see his head

exiting as his tail continues in.
Neither of us fears the other,
such a blessing.
We continue down, knocking loose
rocks and dirt as we go. You mention

the wildlife who trek here, label droppings
along the way. We arrive at the canyon
floor intact. When I look back
the ledge disappears, blends into red rock,
only a line, a scratch on the cliff,

though I can make out the stone
pointing the path. We cross to the arroyo,
dip in, rise up again while you narrate
from your life in Costa Rica.
But I am thinking about snakes,

which are numerous, you tell me,
in Costa Rica, about dangerous
myths, about my grandmother's hoe
raised high over her head, the black snake
doomed to be chopped in half.

Frog Moon

What was it that made me hear
my name, struck
like a drum,
as I lay sleeping alone
in the pod of the old adobe

and rise to open the window
on the shoreline
of dreams?

What was it there, croaking
in the dark pond of night,
puffed up like a crystal ball,
full of knowledge and mystery

but not talking?

While you napped,
down here someone lit
another cigarette,

someone opened a door,

someone tried to catch your eye.
Was it you who called
my name, frog moon,

as I paddled my canoe
along the rivers of sleep?

Was it you who woke me
to this liquid black,
the rising tide of the Milky Way,

your leap
into the murky waters of night

that leaves me
splashed with stars?

Footnotes

The birds write
their winged history
in the snow
outside my sliding doors,
busy marks
I can't interpret:
arrows and carrots,
vectors and cross stitch,
golf tee impressions,
and a quick Chinese brush stroke
halted half-ideograph.
The story starts
high up (what else,
for birds?)
on the left, just a few
tracks as though one claw
struggled to start
this tale, the first
bird scratching,
the first syllable of flight.
Lines continue,
rhyming (I can tell by the loose
swirl of the circle, the doubling back
of the double track), the first epic
transcribed from chirping.
I follow the trails
which divide in all directions,
till the right side
of the text ends

in pencilled chatter.
Just now a single bird lights
at the far corner, pecks
two annotations,
flies away
from this curious bird-talk
air mailed
to my back yard.

Buffalo Sky

I stop at the window to watch clouds
shift over the lake. They come
from the north, shaggy, clumps
of upper atmosphere, and behind them
the gold tongue of sunset, the horizon
alight, prairie fire thin like wire
around them. The clouds gallop,
pick up speed, take on weight:
hundreds of lumbering bison
their hooves singing

elegy, so many of them, clouds
jostling me, the scuff and gravel
of their ghost retreat, pounding
indentations in the sky's highway
as they charge forward against wind,
become wind, thundering south
like the light-winged Canada geese
while I am left, behind glass,
dust in my throat, with the moon
wide-eyed, ready to bolt.

Witness

Dusk, and with two slices
of old bread I go to the water
looking for the ducks, hoping
they're looking for me.

Across the lake the voices
of two men about to motor off
in a rowboat carry my way.
They are talking about

the plentiful blue gill,
how many they will catch.
Along the narrow inlet
the Canada geese preen

and nibble at careless movements
in twig and moss. When I toss
bread into the water, they
will not come. I quack,

noticing a woman on the dock
by her house notice me.
From beneath the boards
one duck lifts off, only

a foot or so above the water,
flaps quacking my way
and hydroplanes to my shoreline.
I can't believe he has flown

straight to me. I tear
small chunks, communion size,
and chuck them beside him.
He gobbles them all, then

starts up the rocky bank
between us, his flat webbed feet
slapping the stones, puckering
like suction cups. I bend

toward him, and he snatches
the crumb from my fingers,
his narrow bill snapping
shut on my thumb, tugging.

He is not afraid. I want
to reach down and ferry him
to the grass, my fingers
floating through his iridescent

feathers, touch the thick fans
of his feet. When I offer
no more bread, he plops
back to the water, circles

like a skater, swims out,
then comes back
as if he knows there's more,
and he's just waiting. He quacks

and jabbers to himself, or perhaps
to me, as he paddles back
toward the dock, and suddenly
I see the dog I loved

in the tilt of his head,
his eager eye, her quirky barking
in his random quacks, something
familiar in his hesitation

to go. She died five years ago,
but made her first return to me
exactly one year later as I slept
in a tent in the Catalina foothills,

coyotes howling around me
all hours of the night.
One voice was different,
was hers, and I knew she'd come back,

a noisy clue in the mystery
about us. Tonight as I walk
the path back to the cabin,
I know she's come again

from exile in web and feather,
saying there is a different
redemption in bread, in water,
as well as in the desert stars,

saying that, when the time comes,
the world will open out like a bright
question: shape of leaf, print
of paw, sinew of light.

Harriet's Cows

roam the pasture of her studio walls –
some in couples, some in herds
and some tranquilly alone.
One purple Holstein throws an orange
shadow, a doppleganger
from a different world of light.
These three float
on the white paper, no grass
below their hooves, no clouds above,
bovine astronauts of the gallery,
unfenced and unafraid.
Over by the window, the largest clump
dressed in their spectator brown
and white, heavy and genial
in their udder bliss, graze in creamy green
flecked with blue twinkles of dessert.
Female peace permeates the room:
their sturdy forms,
their inscrutable eyes, their ears
cocked and listening
toward the brush.

The Blue Giraffe

On a shelf at Jackalope's
the giraffe with the blue hooves

gathers
with Oaxacan frogs and cats,

fanciful creatures with horns
and wings not invited on

Noah's voyage, an armadillo
built like the ark itself,

fat rabbits and a tiger
that's mostly teeth.

The giraffe with the blue hooves
stands, legs spread like a shortstop's,

head swivelled up,
the long neck rising cobra-like

above the clutter of carvings.
It's amazing, but I see first

those hooves, blue as a child's sky,
then the purple body spotted

with O'Keeffe clouds, the yellow nose
a sun in this off-beat scene.

Her gaze turns up,
never toward customers pawing

menageries of wild color
for one pet to take home.

I buy her because she never looks
my way, her eyes steady

and heavenward, like a coyote
I met on a New Mexico mesa

talking
to shooting stars.

Despite the Ark

You phone from work to say, *Look out
the west window,* a call that brings me
inside from the back deck
where, in the drainpipe, I hear
frantic claws, something scratching
for its life. I stand on the rickety chair
under the guttering but cannot see
or reach down through the top,
can only take the downspout in my hands
and shake, squeeze, try to dislodge
whatever small body struggles
in the metallic dark, reaching
my arm farther up, then bending my wrist
into the elbowed opening, the coolness,
hoping for the bristle of fur or the grip
of a damp paw, not the panic
of teeth. The phone rings
and rings and rings as I climb down,
break into the house to lift the receiver
from its cradle, to say
*someone, help, I can't
get it out* and hear you say,
*Look out the west window. Go
see if it's still there.*
I turn back to the deck and see
arcing over the white pines
a faint rainbow, color drained,
dark clouds thumping against
the sky's tin roof.

Watching the Ducks Return

To land like that,
to come in low over the silvery
airstrip,

webbed feet
swung forward in an arc that brakes
the body,

ripping open
like a zipper the heart
of the lake,

to feel
its beating, beating, beating
against feather

and wing
which flew true
to their mark,

to be held
in the lap and cup, wrinkle and fold
of the lake's skin,

to drop
like a rare coin into the water's
gloved hand

and rest there,
precious and glinting.

So Close

This morning the trees have stopped sighing,
stopped rocking, ceased shaking
their sky-bound heads which,
on the ends of slender
white necks, shook
no no no no all night

as I, too, tossed in the moonless
dark, in the tight air. In my dream,
a young woman I loved
in adolescence galloped along
this beach on a horse that flicked
water from his hooves like loose stars,

like liquid change, like a shattered
vase of light. I felt the slivers
prick my face, but she did not see
me, near enough to hear the horse's
teeth bite air. Before sleep,
walking the dogs on the beach,

I watched five Canada geese
nod on the swell near the shore
when the dogs spied their small fleet.
They hit the water in quick release,
only their furry heads visible
as the geese headed out to sea,

the dogs forgetting their legs
weren't fins. Once I lost a dog
to drowning. My heart swam
with these dogs through the choppy
water, tugging at their names,
trying to herd them back to shore,

and when they both turned, finally,
though the geese with their winged surprise
urged them on, I found myself
waist deep in waves, arms extended
in magnetic hope, trying to pull
all things forgotten from the deep.

Anita Skeen

Anita Skeen is currently Professor of English at Michigan State University where she teaches Creative Writing, Women's Studies, and Canadian Studies. She also serves as the Director of the Residential Option in Arts and Letters Program (ROIAL), a residential living and learning program for selected freshmen and sophomores in the College of Arts and Letters. Before coming to Michigan State in 1990, she was for 18 years on the faculty of the English Department and MFA Program at Wichita State University where she taught creative writing, literature, and Women's Studies. She served on the Board of Directors for the Kansas Humanities Council, participated in the Artists-in-the-Schools Program sponsored by the Kansas Arts Commission, and founded, with Kay Closson, the Kay Closson Women Writing Series at Wichita State. She received her MA and MFA from Bowling Green State University and her BS from Concord College in Athens, West Virginia. She is the author of three volumes of poetry, *Each Hand A Map, Portraits,* and *Outside the Fold, Outside the Frame* and her poetry, short fiction, and essays have appeared in numerous literary magazines and anthologies. She is currently completing a new volume of poetry, a collection of short stories, and a first novel, *Minor Chords.* She is the Director of the Creative Arts Festival at Ghost Ranch Conference Center each June and of the October Writing Festival at Ghost Ranch.